50 Peruvian Dinner Recipes for Home

By: Kelly Johnson

Table of Contents

- Lomo Saltado
- Ceviche
- Aji de Gallina
- Arroz con Pollo
- Anticuchos
- Papa a la Huancaina
- Seco de Cordero
- Rocoto Relleno
- Tiradito
- Causa Limeña
- Adobo de Cerdo
- Chupe de Camarones
- Pollo a la Brasa
- Escabeche de Pescado
- Tacu Tacu
- Carapulcra
- Rocoto Relleno
- Estofado de Pollo
- Olluquito con Charqui
- Parihuela
- Pescado a lo Macho
- Tallarines Verdes
- Solterito de Quinoa
- Chicharrón de Pescado
- Pachamanca
- Chupe de Olluco
- Picante de Mariscos
- Jalea de Mariscos
- Huatia
- Patacones con Pollo
- Tacacho con Cecina
- Mazamorra Morada
- Suspiro a la Limeña
- Mazamorra de Calabaza
- Leche Asada

- Turrón de Doña Pepa
- Alfajores
- Picarones
- Frejol Colado
- Cau Cau
- Tacacho con Cuy
- Arroz Zambito
- Mazamorra de Quinua
- Ensalada de Pallares
- Tamales Peruanos
- Ensalada de Chonta
- Crema Volteada
- Sopa a la Criolla
- Yuca a la Huancaína
- Pisco Sour

Lomo Saltado

Ingredients:

- 1 lb (450g) sirloin steak, thinly sliced
- 2 tablespoons soy sauce
- 2 tablespoons red wine vinegar
- 2 cloves garlic, minced
- 1 teaspoon ground cumin
- Salt and pepper to taste
- 2 tablespoons vegetable oil
- 1 onion, thinly sliced
- 2 tomatoes, sliced into wedges
- 1 yellow chili pepper (aji amarillo), seeded and thinly sliced (optional)
- 1/4 cup chopped fresh cilantro
- 2 tablespoons chopped green onions
- Cooked white rice, for serving
- French fries or boiled potatoes, for serving

Instructions:

1. In a bowl, combine the soy sauce, red wine vinegar, minced garlic, ground cumin, salt, and pepper. Add the sliced sirloin steak to the marinade, cover, and refrigerate for at least 30 minutes, or up to 2 hours.
2. Heat 1 tablespoon of vegetable oil in a large skillet or wok over high heat. Remove the steak from the marinade (reserving the marinade) and add it to the hot skillet. Stir-fry the steak until browned and cooked to your liking, about 3-4 minutes. Remove the steak from the skillet and set aside.
3. In the same skillet, add the remaining 1 tablespoon of vegetable oil. Add the sliced onions and cook until they are soft and lightly browned, about 2-3 minutes.
4. Add the tomato wedges and sliced yellow chili pepper (if using) to the skillet and cook for another 2 minutes, until the tomatoes are slightly softened.
5. Return the cooked steak to the skillet, along with any juices that have accumulated. Pour the reserved marinade over the steak and vegetables. Stir-fry for another 1-2 minutes, until everything is heated through and well combined.
6. Remove the skillet from the heat and stir in the chopped cilantro and green onions.

7. Serve the Lomo Saltado hot, accompanied by cooked white rice and French fries or boiled potatoes.

Enjoy your delicious Peruvian Lomo Saltado!

Ceviche

Ingredients:

- 1 lb (450g) fresh white fish fillets (such as sea bass, sole, or halibut), cut into bite-sized pieces
- 4-5 limes, juiced
- 1 red onion, thinly sliced
- 1-2 fresh chili peppers (such as aji amarillo or rocoto), seeded and thinly sliced (adjust to taste)
- 1-2 garlic cloves, minced
- 1-2 tablespoons chopped fresh cilantro
- Salt and pepper to taste
- 1-2 ears of corn, boiled and sliced (optional)
- 1-2 sweet potatoes, boiled and sliced (optional)
- Lettuce leaves, for serving

Instructions:

1. Place the bite-sized fish pieces in a large glass or ceramic bowl. Make sure the fish is fresh and of high quality.
2. Pour the freshly squeezed lime juice over the fish, making sure it is completely submerged. The acid in the lime juice will "cook" the fish, turning it opaque and firm.
3. Add the thinly sliced red onion, chili peppers, minced garlic, chopped cilantro, salt, and pepper to the bowl with the fish. Gently toss to combine, ensuring that the fish is evenly coated with the marinade.
4. Cover the bowl with plastic wrap and refrigerate for at least 30 minutes to allow the flavors to meld together and the fish to marinate. You can refrigerate it for longer if you prefer a firmer texture.
5. Just before serving, taste the ceviche and adjust the seasoning if necessary.
6. To serve, line serving plates or bowls with lettuce leaves. Spoon the ceviche onto the lettuce leaves, making sure to include some of the marinade. Garnish with slices of boiled corn and sweet potatoes, if using.
7. Serve immediately as an appetizer or light main course, accompanied by crispy corn tortillas, corn nuts, or plantain chips.

Enjoy your refreshing and delicious Peruvian Ceviche!

Aji de Gallina

Ingredients:

- 1 lb (450g) boneless, skinless chicken breasts or thighs
- 2 tablespoons vegetable oil
- 1 onion, finely chopped
- 2 cloves garlic, minced
- 2-3 yellow chili peppers (aji amarillo), seeded and finely chopped (adjust to taste)
- 1 cup chicken broth
- 1 cup evaporated milk or heavy cream
- 4-6 slices white bread, crusts removed
- 1 cup grated Parmesan cheese (or a combination of Parmesan and white cheese like queso fresco)
- Salt and pepper to taste
- 4-6 boiled yellow potatoes, sliced
- Cooked white rice, for serving
- Hard-boiled eggs, sliced, for garnish
- Black olives, for garnish
- Chopped fresh parsley or cilantro, for garnish

Instructions:

1. In a large pot, bring salted water to a boil. Add the chicken breasts or thighs and cook until tender, about 20-25 minutes. Remove the chicken from the pot, let it cool slightly, and then shred it into bite-sized pieces using two forks or your fingers. Reserve the cooking liquid.
2. In a large skillet or saucepan, heat the vegetable oil over medium heat. Add the chopped onion and cook until softened and translucent, about 3-4 minutes. Add the minced garlic and chopped yellow chili peppers and cook for another 2 minutes, stirring frequently.
3. Pour in the chicken broth and evaporated milk (or heavy cream) and stir to combine. Bring the mixture to a simmer.
4. Meanwhile, soak the slices of white bread in the reserved cooking liquid from the chicken until softened. Squeeze out any excess liquid and add the soaked bread to the skillet, stirring until it dissolves into the sauce.

5. Add the shredded chicken to the skillet and stir to coat it evenly with the sauce. Allow the mixture to simmer gently for 5-10 minutes to thicken slightly.
6. Stir in the grated Parmesan cheese (or combination of cheeses) until melted and well incorporated into the sauce. Season with salt and pepper to taste.
7. To serve, arrange the sliced boiled potatoes on individual plates or a serving platter. Spoon the Aji de Gallina over the potatoes and garnish with slices of hard-boiled eggs, black olives, and chopped parsley or cilantro.
8. Serve hot alongside cooked white rice.

Enjoy the rich and flavorful Aji de Gallina!

Arroz con Pollo

Ingredients:

- 2 lbs (about 1 kg) chicken pieces (such as thighs, drumsticks, or breast), skin-on and bone-in
- Salt and pepper to taste
- 2 tablespoons vegetable oil
- 1 onion, finely chopped
- 3 cloves garlic, minced
- 1 red bell pepper, diced
- 1 green bell pepper, diced
- 1 cup frozen peas
- 1 cup corn kernels (fresh, canned, or frozen)
- 2 cups long-grain white rice, rinsed and drained
- 4 cups chicken broth
- 1 teaspoon ground cumin
- 1 teaspoon paprika
- 1/2 teaspoon turmeric
- 1/2 teaspoon dried oregano
- 1 bay leaf
- Fresh cilantro or parsley, chopped, for garnish
- Lime wedges, for serving

Instructions:

1. Season the chicken pieces generously with salt and pepper on both sides.
2. In a large skillet or Dutch oven, heat the vegetable oil over medium-high heat. Add the chicken pieces, skin side down, and cook until golden brown, about 5-7 minutes per side. Remove the chicken from the skillet and set aside.
3. In the same skillet, add the chopped onion, minced garlic, diced red and green bell peppers, frozen peas, and corn kernels. Cook, stirring occasionally, until the vegetables are softened, about 5 minutes.
4. Add the rinsed and drained rice to the skillet and stir to coat it evenly with the vegetables and oil.
5. Pour in the chicken broth and add the ground cumin, paprika, turmeric, dried oregano, and bay leaf. Stir well to combine.

6. Return the browned chicken pieces to the skillet, nestling them into the rice mixture. Bring the mixture to a boil, then reduce the heat to low, cover, and simmer for 20-25 minutes, or until the rice is tender and the chicken is cooked through.
7. Once the rice is cooked, remove the skillet from the heat and let it sit, covered, for 5-10 minutes to allow the flavors to meld together.
8. To serve, garnish the Arroz con Pollo with chopped fresh cilantro or parsley and serve with lime wedges on the side.

Enjoy this comforting and flavorful Peruvian Arroz con Pollo with your favorite side dishes!

Anticuchos

Ingredients:

- 1 lb (450g) beef heart or beef sirloin, cut into bite-sized pieces
- 1/4 cup red wine vinegar
- 2 cloves garlic, minced
- 1 teaspoon ground cumin
- 1 teaspoon paprika
- 1/2 teaspoon dried oregano
- 1/2 teaspoon ground black pepper
- 1/4 teaspoon ground turmeric (optional, for color)
- Salt to taste
- 1-2 tablespoons vegetable oil, for grilling
- Wooden skewers, soaked in water for at least 30 minutes

Instructions:

1. If using beef heart, trim away any excess fat and tough membranes. Cut the beef heart (or beef sirloin) into bite-sized pieces and place them in a large bowl.
2. In a separate bowl, combine the red wine vinegar, minced garlic, ground cumin, paprika, dried oregano, ground black pepper, ground turmeric (if using), and salt to taste. Mix well to combine.
3. Pour the marinade over the beef pieces, ensuring they are evenly coated. Cover the bowl with plastic wrap and refrigerate for at least 2 hours, or preferably overnight, to allow the flavors to develop.
4. Preheat your grill to medium-high heat.
5. Thread the marinated beef pieces onto the soaked wooden skewers, leaving a little space between each piece.
6. Brush the grill grates with vegetable oil to prevent sticking. Place the skewers on the preheated grill and cook for 2-3 minutes per side, or until the meat is cooked through and charred in spots.
7. Remove the skewers from the grill and let them rest for a few minutes before serving.
8. Serve the Anticuchos hot, garnished with additional chopped fresh cilantro or parsley, if desired. They are often accompanied by boiled potatoes or slices of toasted bread.

Enjoy the delicious and flavorful Peruvian Anticuchos as a snack or appetizer!

Papa a la Huancaina

Ingredients:

- 4 large yellow potatoes (such as Yukon Gold), peeled and halved
- 1 cup crumbled queso fresco or feta cheese
- 2-3 yellow chili peppers (aji amarillo), seeded and deveined
- 2 cloves garlic, minced
- 1/2 cup evaporated milk
- 2 tablespoons vegetable oil
- Salt and pepper to taste
- 4-6 lettuce leaves, for serving
- 4-6 hard-boiled eggs, peeled and halved, for serving
- Black olives, for garnish
- Chopped fresh parsley or cilantro, for garnish

Instructions:

1. Place the halved potatoes in a large pot of salted water. Bring to a boil and cook until the potatoes are fork-tender, about 15-20 minutes. Drain the potatoes and set aside to cool slightly.
2. In a blender or food processor, combine the crumbled queso fresco or feta cheese, seeded and deveined yellow chili peppers, minced garlic, evaporated milk, and vegetable oil. Blend until smooth and creamy. If the sauce is too thick, you can add more evaporated milk to achieve the desired consistency. Season with salt and pepper to taste.
3. Slice the cooled potatoes into thick slices and arrange them on a serving platter lined with lettuce leaves.
4. Pour the Huancaina sauce over the sliced potatoes, covering them evenly.
5. Garnish the Papa a la Huancaina with halved hard-boiled eggs and black olives.
6. Sprinkle chopped fresh parsley or cilantro over the top for additional flavor and color.
7. Serve the Papa a la Huancaina at room temperature or chilled.

Enjoy this delicious and creamy Peruvian appetizer or light meal!

Seco de Cordero

Ingredients:

- 2 lbs (about 900g) lamb or goat meat, cut into bite-sized pieces
- 2 tablespoons vegetable oil
- 1 onion, finely chopped
- 3 cloves garlic, minced
- 2 tablespoons aji amarillo paste (yellow chili pepper paste)
- 1 teaspoon ground cumin
- 1 teaspoon ground coriander
- 1/2 teaspoon dried oregano
- Salt and pepper to taste
- 2 cups chicken or beef broth
- 1 cup chopped fresh cilantro leaves and stems
- 2 large potatoes, peeled and cut into chunks
- Cooked white rice, for serving
- Cooked beans (such as canary beans or black beans), for serving

Instructions:

1. Heat the vegetable oil in a large pot or Dutch oven over medium heat. Add the chopped onion and cook until softened and translucent, about 3-4 minutes.
2. Add the minced garlic and aji amarillo paste to the pot, and cook for another 2 minutes, stirring frequently.
3. Season the lamb or goat meat with ground cumin, ground coriander, dried oregano, salt, and pepper. Add the seasoned meat to the pot and brown it on all sides, about 5-7 minutes.
4. Pour in the chicken or beef broth, scraping the bottom of the pot to release any browned bits. Bring the mixture to a simmer, then reduce the heat to low, cover, and let it cook for about 1 hour, or until the meat is tender.
5. Once the meat is tender, stir in the chopped fresh cilantro and add the chunks of peeled potatoes to the pot. Cover and continue to cook until the potatoes are fork-tender, about 15-20 minutes.
6. Taste and adjust the seasoning with salt and pepper if needed.
7. Serve the Seco de Cordero hot, accompanied by cooked white rice and beans.

Enjoy this hearty and flavorful Peruvian stew!

Rocoto Relleno

Ingredients:

- 6-8 large rocoto peppers
- Water
- Salt
- 1 lb (about 450g) ground beef or pork
- 1 onion, finely chopped
- 2 cloves garlic, minced
- 1 tablespoon vegetable oil
- 1 tablespoon aji panca paste (Peruvian red pepper paste) or paprika
- 1 teaspoon ground cumin
- Salt and pepper to taste
- 1/2 cup chopped fresh parsley or cilantro
- 1/2 cup grated Parmesan cheese
- 1/2 cup grated mozzarella cheese or other melting cheese
- Olive oil, for drizzling

Instructions:

1. Begin by preparing the rocoto peppers. Carefully cut off the tops of the peppers and remove the seeds and veins. Rinse the peppers thoroughly under cold water to remove any remaining seeds and spice.
2. In a large pot, bring water to a boil and add a generous amount of salt. Add the cleaned rocoto peppers to the boiling water and cook for about 5 minutes. This step helps to reduce the spiciness of the peppers. Remove the peppers from the water and set aside.
3. Preheat your oven to 350°F (175°C).
4. In a skillet, heat the vegetable oil over medium heat. Add the chopped onion and minced garlic, and sauté until softened and translucent, about 3-4 minutes.
5. Add the ground beef or pork to the skillet and cook until browned, breaking it up with a spoon as it cooks.
6. Stir in the aji panca paste (or paprika), ground cumin, salt, and pepper to taste. Cook for another 2-3 minutes, then remove the skillet from the heat.
7. Stir in the chopped fresh parsley or cilantro, grated Parmesan cheese, and grated mozzarella cheese. Mix until well combined.

8. Stuff each prepared rocoto pepper with the meat and cheese filling, pressing down gently to pack it in.
9. Place the stuffed rocoto peppers in a baking dish. Drizzle with a little olive oil and cover the dish with aluminum foil.
10. Bake in the preheated oven for about 30 minutes, or until the peppers are tender and the filling is heated through.
11. Remove the foil and sprinkle additional grated cheese on top of each stuffed pepper. Return the dish to the oven and bake for another 5-10 minutes, or until the cheese is melted and bubbly.
12. Serve the Rocoto Relleno hot, accompanied by boiled potatoes and aji sauce if desired.

Enjoy the bold flavors of this delicious Peruvian dish!

Tiradito

Ingredients:

- 1 lb (450g) fresh white fish fillets (such as sea bass, sole, or halibut), thinly sliced
- 1/2 cup freshly squeezed lime juice
- 2-3 garlic cloves, minced
- 1-2 aji amarillo peppers, seeded and finely chopped (adjust to taste)
- Salt to taste
- 1 tablespoon vegetable oil
- 1 tablespoon chopped fresh cilantro or parsley, for garnish
- Thinly sliced red onion, for garnish
- Thinly sliced aji amarillo or other chili peppers, for garnish (optional)
- Choclo (Peruvian corn), cancha (toasted corn kernels), or sweet potato, for serving (optional)

Instructions:

1. Place the thinly sliced fish in a shallow dish or on a serving platter, arranging it in a single layer.
2. In a bowl, combine the freshly squeezed lime juice, minced garlic, finely chopped aji amarillo peppers, and salt to taste. Stir well to combine.
3. Pour the lime juice mixture over the sliced fish, ensuring that all the pieces are coated. Let the fish marinate in the refrigerator for about 5-10 minutes.
4. Just before serving, drizzle the vegetable oil over the marinated fish.
5. Garnish the Tiradito with chopped fresh cilantro or parsley, thinly sliced red onion, and thinly sliced aji amarillo or other chili peppers if desired.
6. Serve the Tiradito immediately as an appetizer or light meal, accompanied by choclo (Peruvian corn), cancha (toasted corn kernels), or slices of sweet potato if desired.

Enjoy the refreshing flavors of this Peruvian Tiradito!

Causa Limeña

Ingredients:

For the Potato Layers:

- 4 large yellow potatoes, peeled and cubed
- 2-3 tablespoons lime juice
- 1-2 tablespoons aji amarillo paste (yellow chili pepper paste)
- Salt to taste

For the Filling:

- 1 can tuna or shredded cooked chicken breast
- 1/2 cup mayonnaise
- 1 tablespoon lime juice
- Salt and pepper to taste

For Garnish:

- Hard-boiled eggs, sliced
- Black olives
- Fresh cilantro or parsley leaves

Instructions:

1. Place the cubed potatoes in a large pot and cover with cold water. Add a generous pinch of salt and bring to a boil. Cook until the potatoes are tender when pierced with a fork, about 15-20 minutes.
2. Drain the cooked potatoes and mash them while still warm until smooth. Add lime juice, aji amarillo paste, and salt to taste, mixing well to incorporate. The mashed potatoes should be flavorful and slightly tangy from the lime juice.
3. In a separate bowl, combine the tuna or shredded chicken with mayonnaise, lime juice, salt, and pepper to taste. Mix until well combined.

4. To assemble the Causa Limeña, line a square or rectangular baking dish with plastic wrap, leaving some overhang on the sides for easy removal later.
5. Spread half of the mashed potato mixture evenly into the bottom of the baking dish, pressing down gently to create a smooth layer.
6. Spread the tuna or chicken filling over the mashed potato layer, smoothing it out with a spatula.
7. Top the filling with the remaining mashed potato mixture, spreading it evenly to cover the filling and create a second layer.
8. Cover the baking dish with plastic wrap and refrigerate for at least 1 hour to allow the Causa Limeña to set and flavors to meld together.
9. Once chilled and set, carefully lift the Causa Limeña out of the baking dish using the overhanging plastic wrap. Transfer it to a serving platter.
10. Garnish the Causa Limeña with slices of hard-boiled eggs, black olives, and fresh cilantro or parsley leaves.
11. Slice the Causa Limeña into squares or rectangles and serve chilled as an appetizer or light meal.

Enjoy the delicious layers of flavor in this traditional Peruvian Causa Limeña!

Adobo de Cerdo

Ingredients:

- 2 lbs (about 900g) pork shoulder or pork loin, cut into bite-sized pieces
- 1/2 cup white vinegar
- 4 cloves garlic, minced
- 1 tablespoon ground cumin
- 1 tablespoon dried oregano
- 1 teaspoon paprika
- 1 teaspoon ground black pepper
- 1 teaspoon salt, or to taste
- 2 tablespoons vegetable oil
- 1 onion, finely chopped
- 1 cup chicken or pork broth
- 2 bay leaves
- Cooked white rice, for serving
- Sliced red onion and chopped fresh cilantro, for garnish (optional)

Instructions:

1. In a large bowl, combine the white vinegar, minced garlic, ground cumin, dried oregano, paprika, ground black pepper, and salt. Stir well to combine.
2. Add the bite-sized pieces of pork to the marinade, making sure they are well coated. Cover the bowl and refrigerate for at least 2 hours, or preferably overnight, to allow the flavors to develop.
3. Heat the vegetable oil in a large pot or Dutch oven over medium-high heat. Add the finely chopped onion and cook until softened and translucent, about 3-4 minutes.
4. Remove the marinated pork from the refrigerator and transfer it to the pot, reserving the marinade. Cook the pork until browned on all sides, about 5-7 minutes.
5. Pour the reserved marinade over the browned pork in the pot. Add the chicken or pork broth and bay leaves. Stir well to combine.
6. Bring the mixture to a simmer, then reduce the heat to low. Cover the pot and let the Adobo de Cerdo simmer gently for about 1 to 1 1/2 hours, stirring occasionally, or until the pork is tender and the flavors have melded together.

7. Taste and adjust the seasoning with salt and pepper if needed.
8. Once the pork is tender, remove the bay leaves from the pot and discard them.
9. Serve the Adobo de Cerdo hot, accompanied by cooked white rice. Garnish with sliced red onion and chopped fresh cilantro if desired.

Enjoy the rich and savory flavors of this traditional Peruvian Adobo de Cerdo!

Chupe de Camarones

Ingredients:

- 1 lb (about 450g) large shrimp, peeled and deveined
- 4 tablespoons vegetable oil
- 1 onion, finely chopped
- 2 cloves garlic, minced
- 1-2 aji amarillo peppers, seeded and finely chopped (adjust to taste)
- 1 teaspoon ground cumin
- 4 cups fish or shrimp stock
- 2 cups diced potatoes
- 1 cup corn kernels (fresh, canned, or frozen)
- 1 cup green peas (fresh or frozen)
- 1 cup evaporated milk
- 1/2 cup heavy cream
- 2 eggs
- 1/4 cup chopped fresh cilantro or parsley
- Salt and pepper to taste
- Lime wedges, for serving
- Sliced hard-boiled eggs, for garnish (optional)
- Sliced black olives, for garnish (optional)

Instructions:

1. In a large pot or Dutch oven, heat the vegetable oil over medium heat. Add the finely chopped onion and cook until softened and translucent, about 3-4 minutes.
2. Add the minced garlic and chopped aji amarillo peppers to the pot, and cook for another 2 minutes, stirring frequently.
3. Stir in the ground cumin and cook for another minute to toast the spices.
4. Pour the fish or shrimp stock into the pot and bring the mixture to a simmer.
5. Add the diced potatoes to the pot and cook until they are just beginning to soften, about 10 minutes.
6. Stir in the corn kernels, green peas, and peeled and deveined shrimp. Cook for another 5-7 minutes, or until the shrimp are pink and cooked through.
7. In a separate bowl, whisk together the evaporated milk, heavy cream, and eggs until well combined.

8. Slowly pour the milk and egg mixture into the pot, stirring constantly to prevent curdling. Cook for another 5 minutes, or until the soup has thickened slightly.
9. Stir in the chopped fresh cilantro or parsley, and season the chowder with salt and pepper to taste.
10. Ladle the Chupe de Camarones into bowls and serve hot, accompanied by lime wedges for squeezing over the soup.
11. Optionally, garnish each bowl with sliced hard-boiled eggs and sliced black olives before serving.

Enjoy the creamy and delicious flavors of this Peruvian Chupe de Camarones!

Pollo a la Brasa

Ingredients:

- 1 whole chicken, about 4-5 lbs (1.8-2.3 kg)
- For the Marinade:
    - 4 cloves garlic, minced
    - 2 tablespoons soy sauce
    - 2 tablespoons vegetable oil
    - 2 tablespoons white vinegar or apple cider vinegar
    - 1 tablespoon paprika
    - 1 tablespoon cumin
    - 1 teaspoon black pepper
    - 1 teaspoon dried oregano
    - 1 teaspoon salt, or to taste
    - Juice of 1 lime or lemon
- For Serving:
    - Aji verde (Peruvian green sauce)
    - French fries or boiled potatoes
    - Salad or coleslaw

Instructions:

1. In a bowl, mix together all the ingredients for the marinade until well combined.
2. Place the whole chicken in a large resealable plastic bag or a shallow dish. Pour the marinade over the chicken, making sure it's evenly coated. Seal the bag or cover the dish and refrigerate for at least 4 hours, or preferably overnight, to allow the flavors to penetrate the meat.
3. Preheat your grill to medium-high heat.
4. Remove the chicken from the marinade and let any excess marinade drip off. Reserve the leftover marinade for basting.
5. If using a charcoal grill, arrange the coals on one side of the grill for indirect heat. If using a gas grill, turn off the burners on one side for indirect heat.
6. Place the chicken on the grill over indirect heat, breast side up. Close the lid and cook for about 1 to 1 1/2 hours, or until the internal temperature of the chicken reaches 165°F (74°C), basting occasionally with the reserved marinade.

7. If using a rotisserie, secure the chicken on the spit and cook according to the manufacturer's instructions, basting occasionally with the marinade.
8. Once the chicken is cooked through and has a golden brown color, remove it from the grill and let it rest for a few minutes before carving.
9. Serve the Pollo a la Brasa hot, accompanied by aji verde (Peruvian green sauce), French fries or boiled potatoes, and salad or coleslaw.

Enjoy the delicious and flavorful Peruvian-style rotisserie chicken!

Escabeche de Pescado

Ingredients:

- 1 lb (about 450g) firm white fish fillets (such as sea bass, tilapia, or halibut), cut into serving-sized pieces
- Salt and pepper to taste
- All-purpose flour, for dusting
- Vegetable oil, for frying
- 1 red onion, thinly sliced
- 1 red bell pepper, thinly sliced
- 1 yellow bell pepper, thinly sliced
- 2 cloves garlic, minced
- 1/2 cup white vinegar
- 1/2 cup water
- 1 teaspoon ground cumin
- 1 teaspoon paprika
- 1 bay leaf
- 1/4 cup chopped fresh cilantro or parsley, for garnish
- Cooked white rice, for serving

Instructions:

1. Season the fish fillets with salt and pepper, then lightly dust them with flour, shaking off any excess.
2. In a large skillet or frying pan, heat enough vegetable oil to cover the bottom of the pan over medium-high heat. Once the oil is hot, add the fish fillets and cook until golden brown and cooked through, about 3-4 minutes per side depending on thickness. Remove the cooked fish from the pan and place them on a plate lined with paper towels to drain any excess oil.
3. In the same skillet or a separate saucepan, heat a tablespoon of vegetable oil over medium heat. Add the thinly sliced onions, bell peppers, and minced garlic, and cook until softened, about 5-7 minutes.
4. In a small bowl, whisk together the white vinegar, water, ground cumin, paprika, and bay leaf.
5. Pour the vinegar mixture over the cooked vegetables in the skillet. Bring the mixture to a simmer and let it cook for another 5 minutes, stirring occasionally.

6. Place the cooked fish fillets in a shallow dish or baking dish, then pour the hot vinegar mixture over the fish, covering them evenly.
7. Cover the dish with plastic wrap or a lid and refrigerate for at least 2 hours, or overnight, to allow the flavors to meld together.
8. Before serving, garnish the Escabeche de Pescado with chopped fresh cilantro or parsley.
9. Serve the Escabeche de Pescado cold or at room temperature, accompanied by cooked white rice.

Enjoy the tangy and flavorful Peruvian Escabeche de Pescado!

Tacu Tacu

Ingredients:

- 2 cups cooked white rice
- 1 cup cooked canary beans or black beans, drained and mashed
- 2 tablespoons vegetable oil
- 1 onion, finely chopped
- 2 cloves garlic, minced
- 1 teaspoon ground cumin
- Salt and pepper to taste
- Additional vegetable oil for frying
- Fried eggs, sliced steak, or seafood for serving (optional)
- Sliced red onions and aji sauce for garnish (optional)

Instructions:

1. In a large bowl, combine the cooked white rice and mashed beans. Use a fork or potato masher to mix them together until well combined. The mixture should be thick and slightly sticky.
2. In a skillet or frying pan, heat the vegetable oil over medium heat. Add the finely chopped onion and minced garlic, and sauté until softened and translucent, about 3-4 minutes.
3. Add the ground cumin to the skillet and cook for another minute, stirring constantly to toast the spice.
4. Add the rice and bean mixture to the skillet, spreading it out evenly in the pan. Let it cook undisturbed for a few minutes to develop a crispy crust on the bottom.
5. Using a spatula, flip the Tacu Tacu over to crisp up the other side. Cook for another 5-7 minutes, or until both sides are golden brown and crispy.
6. Season the Tacu Tacu with salt and pepper to taste, then remove it from the skillet and transfer it to a serving platter.
7. In the same skillet, fry the eggs, steak, or seafood if using, until cooked to your liking.
8. Serve the Tacu Tacu hot, topped with the fried eggs, steak, or seafood if desired. Garnish with sliced red onions and aji sauce if desired.

Enjoy the delicious and comforting flavors of this classic Peruvian Tacu Tacu!

Carapulcra

Ingredients:

- 1 lb (about 450g) pork shoulder, chicken thighs, or beef stew meat, cut into bite-sized pieces
- 1 cup dried potatoes (papa seca), soaked in water overnight and drained
- 2 tablespoons vegetable oil
- 1 onion, finely chopped
- 2 cloves garlic, minced
- 2 tablespoons aji panca paste (Peruvian red pepper paste)
- 1 tablespoon ground cumin
- 1 teaspoon dried oregano
- 1/2 teaspoon ground cloves
- 1/2 teaspoon ground cinnamon
- 1/2 cup white wine or pisco (Peruvian grape brandy)
- 4 cups chicken or beef broth
- Salt and pepper to taste
- Chopped fresh cilantro or parsley, for garnish
- Cooked white rice, for serving

Instructions:

1. In a large pot or Dutch oven, heat the vegetable oil over medium-high heat. Add the chopped onion and minced garlic, and cook until softened and translucent, about 3-4 minutes.
2. Add the aji panca paste to the pot and cook for another 2 minutes, stirring constantly to prevent burning.
3. Add the pork, chicken, or beef to the pot and cook until browned on all sides, about 5-7 minutes.
4. Stir in the soaked dried potatoes, ground cumin, dried oregano, ground cloves, and ground cinnamon. Cook for another 2-3 minutes to toast the spices.
5. Pour in the white wine or pisco, scraping the bottom of the pot to deglaze and loosen any browned bits.
6. Add the chicken or beef broth to the pot and bring the mixture to a simmer. Cover and cook over low heat for about 1 hour, or until the meat is tender and the potatoes are fully rehydrated.

7. Season the Carapulcra with salt and pepper to taste.
8. Serve the Carapulcra hot, garnished with chopped fresh cilantro or parsley. Accompany with cooked white rice.

Enjoy the rich and hearty flavors of this traditional Peruvian Carapulcra!

Rocoto Relleno

Ingredients:

- 6-8 large rocoto peppers
- Water
- Salt
- 1 lb (about 450g) ground beef or pork
- 1 onion, finely chopped
- 2 cloves garlic, minced
- 1 tablespoon vegetable oil
- 1 tablespoon aji panca paste (Peruvian red pepper paste) or paprika
- 1 teaspoon ground cumin
- 1 teaspoon dried oregano
- Salt and pepper to taste
- 1/2 cup grated Parmesan cheese
- 1/2 cup grated mozzarella cheese or other melting cheese
- Olive oil, for drizzling

Instructions:

1. Begin by preparing the rocoto peppers. Carefully cut off the tops of the peppers and remove the seeds and veins. Rinse the peppers thoroughly under cold water to remove any remaining seeds and spice. To reduce the spiciness, soak the prepared peppers in salted water for about 30 minutes, then rinse again.
2. Preheat your oven to 350°F (175°C).
3. In a skillet, heat the vegetable oil over medium heat. Add the chopped onion and minced garlic, and sauté until softened and translucent, about 3-4 minutes.
4. Add the ground beef or pork to the skillet and cook until browned, breaking it up with a spoon as it cooks.
5. Stir in the aji panca paste (or paprika), ground cumin, dried oregano, salt, and pepper to taste. Cook for another 2-3 minutes, then remove the skillet from the heat.
6. Stir in the grated Parmesan cheese and grated mozzarella cheese until well combined.
7. Stuff each prepared rocoto pepper with the meat and cheese filling, pressing down gently to pack it in.

8. Place the stuffed rocoto peppers in a baking dish. Drizzle with a little olive oil.
9. Cover the baking dish with aluminum foil and bake in the preheated oven for about 30-40 minutes, or until the peppers are tender.
10. Remove the foil and sprinkle additional grated cheese on top of each stuffed pepper. Return the dish to the oven and bake for another 5-10 minutes, or until the cheese is melted and bubbly.
11. Serve the Rocoto Relleno hot, accompanied by boiled potatoes or slices of toasted bread.

Enjoy the bold flavors of this delicious Peruvian Rocoto Relleno!

Estofado de Pollo

Ingredients:

- 2 lbs (about 900g) chicken pieces (such as thighs, drumsticks, or breasts), bone-in and skin-on
- Salt and pepper to taste
- 2 tablespoons vegetable oil
- 1 onion, finely chopped
- 2 cloves garlic, minced
- 1 bell pepper (red or green), diced
- 2 tomatoes, diced
- 1 tablespoon tomato paste
- 1 teaspoon ground cumin
- 1 teaspoon paprika
- 1/2 teaspoon dried oregano
- 2 cups chicken broth
- 2 large potatoes, peeled and cut into chunks
- 2 carrots, peeled and sliced
- 1 cup frozen peas
- Chopped fresh cilantro or parsley, for garnish
- Cooked white rice or crusty bread, for serving

Instructions:

1. Season the chicken pieces with salt and pepper to taste.
2. In a large pot or Dutch oven, heat the vegetable oil over medium-high heat. Add the chicken pieces and brown them on all sides, about 5-7 minutes. Remove the chicken from the pot and set it aside.
3. In the same pot, add the chopped onion, minced garlic, and diced bell pepper. Sauté until the vegetables are softened, about 3-4 minutes.
4. Add the diced tomatoes and tomato paste to the pot, stirring to combine. Cook for another 2-3 minutes.
5. Stir in the ground cumin, paprika, and dried oregano, and cook for another minute to toast the spices.

6. Return the browned chicken pieces to the pot, along with any juices that have accumulated. Pour in the chicken broth, ensuring that the chicken is submerged in the liquid.
7. Bring the mixture to a simmer, then reduce the heat to low. Cover the pot and let it simmer gently for about 30 minutes, or until the chicken is cooked through and tender.
8. Add the peeled and chopped potatoes, sliced carrots, and frozen peas to the pot. Stir to combine.
9. Cover the pot again and let the stew simmer for another 20-25 minutes, or until the vegetables are tender and the flavors have melded together.
10. Taste and adjust the seasoning with salt and pepper if needed.
11. Serve the Estofado de Pollo hot, garnished with chopped fresh cilantro or parsley. Accompany with cooked white rice or crusty bread.

Enjoy the comforting and delicious flavors of this Peruvian Estofado de Pollo!

Olluquito con Charqui

Ingredients:

- 1 lb (about 450g) olluco, peeled and sliced into thin rounds
- 1/2 lb (about 225g) charqui (dried meat), thinly sliced or shredded
- 2 tablespoons vegetable oil
- 1 onion, finely chopped
- 2 cloves garlic, minced
- 1 tomato, diced
- 1 tablespoon aji amarillo paste (Peruvian yellow chili pepper paste)
- 1 teaspoon ground cumin
- 1/2 teaspoon dried oregano
- Salt and pepper to taste
- 2 cups beef or vegetable broth
- 2 medium potatoes, peeled and cut into chunks
- 1 carrot, peeled and sliced
- 1/2 cup frozen peas
- Cooked white rice, for serving
- Chopped fresh cilantro or parsley, for garnish

Instructions:

1. If using charqui (dried meat), soak it in warm water for about 30 minutes to rehydrate. Once rehydrated, drain the charqui and shred or thinly slice it.
2. In a large pot or Dutch oven, heat the vegetable oil over medium heat. Add the chopped onion and minced garlic, and sauté until softened and translucent, about 3-4 minutes.
3. Add the diced tomato and aji amarillo paste to the pot, stirring to combine. Cook for another 2-3 minutes.
4. Stir in the ground cumin, dried oregano, salt, and pepper to taste. Cook for another minute to toast the spices.
5. Add the sliced olluco and shredded or thinly sliced charqui to the pot, stirring to coat them with the onion and spice mixture.
6. Pour in the beef or vegetable broth, ensuring that the olluco and charqui are submerged in the liquid. Bring the mixture to a simmer.

7. Add the peeled and chopped potatoes, sliced carrot, and frozen peas to the pot, stirring to combine.
8. Cover the pot and let the stew simmer gently for about 20-25 minutes, or until the olluco and vegetables are tender and cooked through.
9. Taste and adjust the seasoning with salt and pepper if needed.
10. Serve the Olluquito con Charqui hot, accompanied by cooked white rice. Garnish with chopped fresh cilantro or parsley.

Enjoy the rich and comforting flavors of this traditional Peruvian dish!

Parihuela

Ingredients:

- 1 lb (about 450g) mixed seafood (such as fish fillets, shrimp, squid, mussels, and/or scallops), cleaned and cut into bite-sized pieces
- 2 tablespoons vegetable oil
- 1 onion, finely chopped
- 2 cloves garlic, minced
- 1 bell pepper (red or green), diced
- 1 tomato, diced
- 2 tablespoons tomato paste
- 1 tablespoon aji amarillo paste (Peruvian yellow chili pepper paste)
- 1 teaspoon ground cumin
- 1/2 teaspoon dried oregano
- 1 bay leaf
- 4 cups fish or seafood broth
- 1 cup clam juice or fish stock
- 1 cup white wine or pisco (Peruvian grape brandy)
- 2 large potatoes, peeled and diced
- 1 cup frozen peas
- Salt and pepper to taste
- Chopped fresh cilantro or parsley, for garnish
- Lime wedges, for serving
- Toasted bread or cooked white rice, for serving

Instructions:

1. In a large pot or Dutch oven, heat the vegetable oil over medium heat. Add the chopped onion and minced garlic, and sauté until softened and translucent, about 3-4 minutes.
2. Add the diced bell pepper and tomato to the pot, stirring to combine. Cook for another 3-4 minutes.
3. Stir in the tomato paste, aji amarillo paste, ground cumin, dried oregano, and bay leaf. Cook for another 2-3 minutes to allow the flavors to meld together.
4. Pour in the fish or seafood broth, clam juice or fish stock, and white wine or pisco. Bring the mixture to a simmer.

5. Add the diced potatoes to the pot and cook until they are just beginning to soften, about 8-10 minutes.
6. Add the mixed seafood to the pot, along with the frozen peas. Let the soup simmer gently for another 5-7 minutes, or until the seafood is cooked through and tender.
7. Taste and adjust the seasoning with salt and pepper if needed.
8. Ladle the Parihuela into bowls and garnish with chopped fresh cilantro or parsley.
9. Serve the Parihuela hot, accompanied by lime wedges for squeezing over the soup. Serve with toasted bread or cooked white rice on the side.

Enjoy the delicious and comforting flavors of this traditional Peruvian seafood soup!

Pescado a lo Macho

Ingredients:

- 4 fish fillets (such as sea bass, sole, or tilapia)
- Salt and pepper to taste
- All-purpose flour, for dusting
- Vegetable oil for frying
- 1 onion, finely chopped
- 2 cloves garlic, minced
- 1 bell pepper (red or yellow), thinly sliced
- 1 tomato, diced
- 1 tablespoon aji amarillo paste (Peruvian yellow chili pepper paste)
- 1/2 cup fish or seafood broth
- 1/2 cup heavy cream or evaporated milk
- 1/2 cup grated Parmesan cheese
- 1/2 cup cooked mixed seafood (such as shrimp, squid, and/or scallops)
- 1 tablespoon chopped fresh cilantro or parsley, for garnish
- Lime wedges, for serving
- Boiled potatoes or yuca, for serving
- Cooked white rice, for serving

Instructions:

1. Season the fish fillets with salt and pepper, then lightly dust them with flour, shaking off any excess.
2. Heat vegetable oil in a large skillet over medium-high heat. Fry the fish fillets until golden brown on both sides and cooked through, about 3-4 minutes per side depending on thickness. Remove the fillets from the skillet and drain on paper towels.
3. In the same skillet, add a little more oil if needed, then sauté the chopped onion, minced garlic, and sliced bell pepper until softened, about 3-4 minutes.
4. Add the diced tomato and aji amarillo paste to the skillet, stirring to combine. Cook for another 2-3 minutes.
5. Pour in the fish or seafood broth and bring the mixture to a simmer.
6. Reduce the heat to low and stir in the heavy cream or evaporated milk. Let the sauce simmer gently for a few minutes to thicken slightly.

7. Stir in the grated Parmesan cheese until melted and well combined.
8. Add the cooked mixed seafood to the skillet, stirring to coat them in the sauce.
9. Return the fried fish fillets to the skillet, spooning some of the sauce over the top.
10. Let the fish simmer in the sauce for another 2-3 minutes to heat through.
11. Taste the sauce and adjust the seasoning with salt and pepper if needed.
12. Garnish the Pescado a lo Macho with chopped fresh cilantro or parsley.
13. Serve the Pescado a lo Macho hot, accompanied by lime wedges, boiled potatoes or yuca, and cooked white rice.

Enjoy the bold and delicious flavors of this Peruvian seafood dish!

Tallarines Verdes

Ingredients:

- 1 lb (about 450g) spaghetti or fettuccine
- Salt for pasta water
- 1 cup fresh basil leaves
- 1 cup fresh spinach leaves
- 2 cloves garlic, minced
- 1/2 cup grated Parmesan cheese
- 1/4 cup grated queso fresco or feta cheese
- 1/2 cup evaporated milk or heavy cream
- 1/4 cup vegetable oil or olive oil
- 1/4 cup walnuts or pine nuts (optional)
- Salt and pepper to taste
- 2 tablespoons butter (optional)
- Grated Parmesan cheese, for serving

Instructions:

1. Bring a large pot of salted water to a boil. Cook the spaghetti or fettuccine according to package instructions until al dente. Drain the pasta, reserving about 1 cup of pasta water, and set aside.
2. In a blender or food processor, combine the fresh basil leaves, fresh spinach leaves, minced garlic, grated Parmesan cheese, grated queso fresco or feta cheese, evaporated milk or heavy cream, vegetable oil or olive oil, and walnuts or pine nuts if using. Blend until smooth and creamy. If the sauce is too thick, you can thin it out with a little pasta water.
3. Heat the butter in a large skillet over medium heat. Once melted, add the green sauce to the skillet and cook for 2-3 minutes, stirring constantly, until heated through and fragrant. Season with salt and pepper to taste.
4. Add the cooked pasta to the skillet with the green sauce and toss until well coated, adding a splash of pasta water if needed to loosen the sauce and help it cling to the pasta.
5. Serve the Tallarines Verdes hot, garnished with grated Parmesan cheese.

Enjoy the vibrant flavors of this classic Peruvian pasta dish!

Solterito de Quinoa

Ingredients:

- 1 cup quinoa
- 2 cups water or vegetable broth
- 1 cup cooked lima beans or fava beans
- 1 cup cooked corn kernels (fresh, canned, or frozen)
- 1 cup diced tomatoes
- 1/2 cup diced red onion
- 1/2 cup diced bell pepper (red, yellow, or green)
- 1/2 cup diced cucumber
- 1/2 cup diced avocado
- 1/2 cup diced fresh cheese (such as queso fresco or feta)
- 1/4 cup chopped fresh cilantro
- Salt and pepper to taste
- Juice of 1 lime
- 2 tablespoons extra virgin olive oil
- Optional: sliced olives or boiled potatoes for serving

Instructions:

1. Rinse the quinoa under cold water to remove any bitterness. In a medium saucepan, combine the quinoa and water or vegetable broth. Bring to a boil, then reduce the heat to low, cover, and simmer for 15-20 minutes, or until the quinoa is tender and the liquid is absorbed. Remove from heat and let it cool.
2. In a large mixing bowl, combine the cooked quinoa, cooked lima beans or fava beans, cooked corn kernels, diced tomatoes, diced red onion, diced bell pepper, diced cucumber, diced avocado, diced fresh cheese, and chopped fresh cilantro. Toss gently to combine.
3. In a small bowl, whisk together the lime juice and extra virgin olive oil to make the dressing. Season with salt and pepper to taste.
4. Pour the dressing over the quinoa salad and toss until everything is evenly coated.
5. Taste and adjust the seasoning if needed. You can also add more lime juice or olive oil if desired.

6. Serve the Solterito de Quinoa chilled or at room temperature, garnished with additional chopped cilantro and sliced olives if desired. You can also serve it with boiled potatoes on the side.

Enjoy the fresh and vibrant flavors of this Peruvian quinoa salad!

Chicharrón de Pescado

Ingredients:

- 1 lb (about 450g) firm white fish fillets (such as sea bass, tilapia, or cod)
- Salt and pepper to taste
- 1/2 cup all-purpose flour
- Vegetable oil for frying
- Lime wedges, for serving
- Salsa criolla (Peruvian onion salsa), for serving (optional)
- Yuca fries or boiled yuca, for serving (optional)

Instructions:

1. Cut the fish fillets into bite-sized pieces and season them with salt and pepper.
2. Place the all-purpose flour in a shallow dish and dredge each piece of fish in the flour, shaking off any excess.
3. In a large skillet or frying pan, heat enough vegetable oil over medium-high heat to cover the bottom of the pan.
4. Once the oil is hot, carefully add the fish pieces to the skillet in batches, making sure not to overcrowd the pan. Fry the fish until golden brown and crispy on all sides, about 3-4 minutes per side depending on the thickness of the fish.
5. Use a slotted spoon to transfer the fried fish to a plate lined with paper towels to drain any excess oil.
6. Serve the Chicharrón de Pescado hot, accompanied by lime wedges for squeezing over the fish. You can also serve it with salsa criolla and yuca fries or boiled yuca on the side.
7. Enjoy the crispy and flavorful Chicharrón de Pescado as a delicious appetizer or main course.

This dish is sure to be a hit with its crunchy exterior and tender, juicy fish inside.

Pachamanca

Ingredients:

- 2 lbs (about 900g) beef, pork, and/or lamb, cut into large chunks
- 1 lb (about 450g) chicken pieces
- 1 lb (about 450g) potatoes, peeled and halved
- 1 lb (about 450g) sweet potatoes, peeled and halved
- 1 lb (about 450g) corn on the cob, husks removed and halved
- 1 lb (about 450g) fava beans or lima beans, shelled
- 1 lb (about 450g) cassava (yuca), peeled and cut into chunks (optional)
- 1/2 cup aji panca paste (Peruvian red pepper paste)
- 1/4 cup aji amarillo paste (Peruvian yellow chili pepper paste)
- 1/4 cup vegetable oil
- 1/4 cup red wine vinegar
- 4 cloves garlic, minced
- 2 tablespoons dried oregano
- 2 tablespoons ground cumin
- Salt and pepper to taste
- Banana leaves or aluminum foil for wrapping

Instructions:

1. In a large bowl, combine the aji panca paste, aji amarillo paste, vegetable oil, red wine vinegar, minced garlic, dried oregano, ground cumin, salt, and pepper to make the marinade.
2. Place the beef, pork, lamb, and chicken pieces in the marinade, ensuring they are well coated. Cover the bowl and marinate in the refrigerator for at least 2 hours, or preferably overnight.
3. Preheat your oven to 350°F (175°C).
4. Prepare a large roasting pan or baking dish lined with banana leaves or aluminum foil.
5. Arrange the marinated meat, potatoes, sweet potatoes, corn on the cob, fava beans or lima beans, and cassava (if using) in the roasting pan.
6. Cover the ingredients with additional banana leaves or aluminum foil, sealing the edges tightly to create a parcel.
7. Place the roasting pan in the preheated oven and cook for about 2-3 hours, or until the meat and vegetables are tender and cooked through.

8. Remove the Pachamanca from the oven and carefully unwrap the parcel.
9. Serve the Pachamanca hot, allowing guests to help themselves to the tender meat and flavorful vegetables.

Enjoy the communal experience and rich flavors of this traditional Peruvian dish!

Chupe de Olluco

Ingredients:

- 1 lb (about 450g) olluco, peeled and sliced into thin rounds
- 2 tablespoons vegetable oil
- 1 onion, finely chopped
- 2 cloves garlic, minced
- 1 bell pepper (red or yellow), diced
- 2 tomatoes, diced
- 4 cups chicken or vegetable broth
- 1 cup evaporated milk or heavy cream
- 1 cup fresh or frozen corn kernels
- 1 cup diced cooked chicken or seafood (optional)
- 1 cup queso fresco or feta cheese, crumbled
- 2 tablespoons chopped fresh cilantro
- Salt and pepper to taste
- Sliced hard-boiled eggs for garnish (optional)
- Aji amarillo paste (Peruvian yellow chili pepper paste) for serving (optional)

Instructions:

1. In a large pot or Dutch oven, heat the vegetable oil over medium heat. Add the chopped onion and minced garlic, and sauté until softened and translucent, about 3-4 minutes.
2. Add the diced bell pepper and tomatoes to the pot, stirring to combine. Cook for another 3-4 minutes, until the vegetables are softened.
3. Stir in the sliced olluco and cook for another 2-3 minutes.
4. Pour in the chicken or vegetable broth and bring the mixture to a simmer. Let it cook for about 10-15 minutes, or until the olluco is tender.
5. Stir in the evaporated milk or heavy cream, along with the corn kernels and diced cooked chicken or seafood if using. Let the soup simmer for another 5-10 minutes.
6. Add the crumbled queso fresco or feta cheese to the soup, stirring until it's melted and well incorporated.
7. Season the Chupe de Olluco with salt and pepper to taste.
8. Remove the pot from the heat and stir in the chopped fresh cilantro.

9. Ladle the soup into bowls and garnish with sliced hard-boiled eggs if desired. Serve hot, with aji amarillo paste on the side for those who want to add extra heat to their soup.

Enjoy the rich and comforting flavors of this traditional Peruvian Chupe de Olluco!

Picante de Mariscos

Ingredients:

- 1 lb (about 450g) mixed seafood (such as shrimp, squid, mussels, and/or scallops), cleaned and deveined
- 2 tablespoons vegetable oil
- 1 onion, finely chopped
- 2 cloves garlic, minced
- 1 bell pepper (red or yellow), diced
- 2 tomatoes, diced
- 2 tablespoons aji panca paste (Peruvian red pepper paste)
- 1 tablespoon aji amarillo paste (Peruvian yellow chili pepper paste)
- 1 teaspoon ground cumin
- 1 teaspoon dried oregano
- 2 cups fish or seafood broth
- 1/2 cup evaporated milk or heavy cream
- 1/4 cup chopped fresh cilantro
- Salt and pepper to taste
- Lime wedges, for serving
- Cooked white rice, for serving

Instructions:

1. In a large pot or Dutch oven, heat the vegetable oil over medium heat. Add the chopped onion and minced garlic, and sauté until softened and translucent, about 3-4 minutes.
2. Add the diced bell pepper and tomatoes to the pot, stirring to combine. Cook for another 3-4 minutes, until the vegetables are softened.
3. Stir in the aji panca paste, aji amarillo paste, ground cumin, and dried oregano. Cook for another 2-3 minutes to allow the flavors to meld together.
4. Pour in the fish or seafood broth and bring the mixture to a simmer.
5. Add the mixed seafood to the pot, stirring to combine. Let the stew simmer gently for about 5-7 minutes, or until the seafood is cooked through and tender.
6. Stir in the evaporated milk or heavy cream, and let the stew simmer for another 2-3 minutes.
7. Taste and adjust the seasoning with salt and pepper if needed.
8. Remove the pot from the heat and stir in the chopped fresh cilantro.

9. Serve the Picante de Mariscos hot, accompanied by lime wedges for squeezing over the stew and cooked white rice on the side.

Enjoy the bold and spicy flavors of this Peruvian seafood stew!

Jalea de Mariscos

Ingredients:

For the seafood:

- 1 lb (about 450g) mixed seafood (such as fish fillets, shrimp, calamari rings, and/or scallops)
- 1 cup all-purpose flour
- 1 teaspoon paprika
- Salt and pepper to taste
- Vegetable oil for frying

For the yuca fries:

- 1 lb (about 450g) yuca, peeled and cut into fries
- Vegetable oil for frying
- Salt to taste

For the salsa criolla:

- 1 red onion, thinly sliced
- 1-2 tomatoes, diced
- 1-2 jalapeño peppers or aji amarillo peppers, thinly sliced
- 1/4 cup chopped cilantro
- Juice of 1-2 limes
- Salt and pepper to taste

For serving:

- Lime wedges
- Aji amarillo sauce or your favorite hot sauce

Instructions:

1. Start by preparing the yuca fries. Rinse the yuca fries under cold water to remove any excess starch. Pat them dry with paper towels.
2. Heat vegetable oil in a deep fryer or large pot to 350°F (175°C). Carefully add the yuca fries to the hot oil in batches, frying until golden brown and crispy, about 5-7 minutes per batch. Remove the fries from the oil and drain on paper towels. Season with salt to taste.
3. Prepare the salsa criolla by combining the thinly sliced red onion, diced tomatoes, sliced jalapeño peppers or aji amarillo peppers, chopped cilantro, and lime juice in a bowl. Season with salt and pepper to taste. Let the salsa criolla marinate while you prepare the seafood.
4. In a shallow dish, mix together the all-purpose flour, paprika, salt, and pepper. Dredge the mixed seafood in the flour mixture, shaking off any excess.
5. Heat vegetable oil in a deep fryer or large pot to 375°F (190°C). Carefully add the dredged seafood to the hot oil in batches, frying until golden brown and crispy, about 2-3 minutes per batch. Remove the fried seafood from the oil and drain on paper towels.
6. Arrange the fried seafood and yuca fries on a serving platter. Serve hot with lime wedges, salsa criolla, and aji amarillo sauce or your favorite hot sauce on the side.
7. Enjoy the crispy and flavorful Jalea de Mariscos as a delicious appetizer or main course!

This dish is sure to impress with its crunchy exterior and tender, juicy seafood inside.

Huatia

Ingredients:

- 2 lbs (about 900g) beef or lamb, cut into large chunks
- 1 lb (about 450g) potatoes, peeled and halved
- 1 lb (about 450g) sweet potatoes, peeled and halved
- 1 lb (about 450g) corn on the cob, husks removed and halved
- 1 lb (about 450g) fava beans or lima beans, shelled
- 1/2 cup fresh cilantro, chopped
- 1/4 cup fresh mint leaves, chopped
- Salt to taste
- Banana leaves or aluminum foil for wrapping
- Large stones for heating

Instructions:

1. Prepare a pit in your backyard or outdoor cooking area. The pit should be deep enough to accommodate the ingredients and large stones for heating.
2. Build a fire in the pit and heat large stones until they are very hot.
3. While the stones are heating, prepare the ingredients. Season the beef or lamb chunks with salt and set aside. Arrange the potatoes, sweet potatoes, corn on the cob, and fava beans or lima beans on a large piece of banana leaf or aluminum foil.
4. Once the stones are hot, carefully place them in the pit to line the bottom.
5. Place the banana leaf or aluminum foil containing the ingredients on top of the hot stones.
6. Cover the ingredients with additional banana leaves or aluminum foil, sealing the edges tightly to create a parcel.
7. Cover the parcel with soil or sand to trap the heat and create a makeshift oven.
8. Allow the ingredients to cook in the earthen oven for several hours, typically 4-6 hours, until the meat is tender and the vegetables are cooked through.
9. Carefully remove the parcel from the pit and uncover the ingredients.
10. Serve the Huatia hot, allowing guests to help themselves to the tender meat and flavorful vegetables.

Enjoy the unique flavors and communal experience of this traditional Andean dish!

Patacones con Pollo

Ingredients:

For the patacones:

- 2 green plantains
- Vegetable oil for frying
- Salt to taste

For the shredded chicken:

- 2 boneless, skinless chicken breasts
- 1 onion, chopped
- 2 cloves garlic, minced
- 1 bell pepper, diced
- 1 tomato, diced
- 1 teaspoon ground cumin
- 1 teaspoon paprika
- Salt and pepper to taste
- 2 cups chicken broth or water
- Vegetable oil for cooking

Optional toppings:

- Salsa criolla (a tangy onion and tomato salsa)
- Guacamole
- Queso fresco or crumbled feta cheese
- Chopped cilantro
- Lime wedges

Instructions:

1. Prepare the shredded chicken: In a large skillet, heat some vegetable oil over medium heat. Add the chopped onion, minced garlic, and diced bell pepper. Sauté until softened, about 3-4 minutes.

2. Add the diced tomato, ground cumin, paprika, salt, and pepper to the skillet. Cook for another 2-3 minutes.
3. Add the chicken breasts to the skillet and pour in the chicken broth or water. Bring to a simmer, then cover and cook until the chicken is cooked through and tender, about 15-20 minutes.
4. Once cooked, remove the chicken from the skillet and shred it using two forks. Return the shredded chicken to the skillet and mix it with the sauce. Keep warm until ready to serve.
5. Prepare the patacones: Peel the green plantains and cut them into thick slices, about 1 inch (2.5 cm) thick.
6. Heat vegetable oil in a large skillet or deep fryer over medium-high heat. Fry the plantain slices until golden brown and crispy, about 2-3 minutes per side. Remove them from the oil and drain on paper towels.
7. Using a flat-bottomed glass or a plantain press, flatten each fried plantain slice into a disc, about 1/4 inch (0.5 cm) thick.
8. Return the flattened plantain discs to the hot oil and fry them again until crispy and golden brown, about 1-2 minutes per side. Remove them from the oil and drain on paper towels. Sprinkle with salt while still hot.
9. To assemble, place a spoonful of shredded chicken on top of each patacone. Add any desired toppings, such as salsa criolla, guacamole, crumbled cheese, chopped cilantro, and lime wedges.
10. Serve the Patacones con Pollo immediately, while still warm and crispy. Enjoy as a delicious appetizer or main dish!

Feel free to customize the toppings to your preference, and enjoy the flavorful combination of crispy patacones and tender shredded chicken.

Tacacho con Cecina

Ingredients:

For the Tacacho:

- 4 green plantains
- Salt to taste
- Vegetable oil for frying

For the Cecina:

- 1 lb (about 450g) beef or pork loin, thinly sliced
- 2 cloves garlic, minced
- 1 tablespoon ground cumin
- 1 tablespoon aji panca paste (Peruvian red pepper paste) or paprika
- Salt and pepper to taste
- Vegetable oil for cooking

Optional garnishes:

- Salsa criolla (a tangy onion and tomato salsa)
- Aji amarillo sauce (Peruvian yellow chili pepper sauce)
- Lime wedges

Instructions:

1. Prepare the Tacacho:
    - Peel the green plantains and cut them into chunks.
    - In a large pot, boil the plantain chunks in salted water until they are fork-tender, about 15-20 minutes.
    - Drain the cooked plantains and transfer them to a large bowl. Mash them using a potato masher or fork until smooth.
    - Season the mashed plantains with salt to taste.

- Shape the mashed plantains into small balls or patties.
2. Heat vegetable oil in a large skillet over medium heat. Fry the Tacacho balls or patties in batches until golden brown and crispy on the outside, about 3-4 minutes per side. Remove them from the oil and drain on paper towels.
3. Prepare the Cecina:
   - In a bowl, combine the minced garlic, ground cumin, aji panca paste or paprika, salt, and pepper to make a marinade.
   - Rub the marinade all over the thinly sliced beef or pork loin, ensuring it's evenly coated. Let it marinate for at least 30 minutes, or overnight in the refrigerator for maximum flavor.
4. Heat vegetable oil in a grill pan or skillet over medium-high heat. Cook the marinated beef or pork slices in batches until cooked through and browned on both sides, about 2-3 minutes per side. Remove them from the heat and let them rest for a few minutes.
5. Serve the Tacacho and Cecina together on a plate. Optionally, garnish with salsa criolla, aji amarillo sauce, and lime wedges.
6. Enjoy Tacacho con Cecina as a flavorful and hearty dish, typically enjoyed as a main course or snack in Peru's Amazon region!

Feel free to adjust the seasoning and spice level according to your taste preferences.

Mazamorra Morada

Ingredients:

- 2 cups purple corn kernels (dried or fresh)
- 8 cups water
- 1 cinnamon stick
- 4 cloves
- 1 cup dried fruit (such as prunes, raisins, and dried apricots)
- 1 cup fresh fruit (such as pineapple, apple, and pear), diced
- 1 cup sugar (adjust to taste)
- 1/4 cup cornstarch
- Juice of 1 lime
- Ground cinnamon for garnish (optional)

Instructions:

1. In a large pot, combine the purple corn kernels, water, cinnamon stick, and cloves. Bring to a boil over medium-high heat.
2. Reduce the heat to low and simmer the mixture, uncovered, for about 1 hour, or until the purple corn kernels are soft and have imparted their color to the water.
3. Strain the mixture through a fine-mesh sieve, discarding the solids (purple corn kernels, cinnamon stick, and cloves). You should be left with a deep purple liquid.
4. Return the purple liquid to the pot and add the dried fruit and fresh fruit. Simmer for another 10-15 minutes, or until the fruit is softened.
5. In a small bowl, dissolve the cornstarch in a little water to make a slurry.
6. Gradually pour the cornstarch slurry into the pot, stirring constantly, until the mixture thickens to your desired consistency.
7. Add the sugar and lime juice to the pot, stirring until the sugar is completely dissolved. Taste and adjust the sweetness if needed.
8. Remove the pot from the heat and let the Mazamorra Morada cool slightly.
9. Transfer the Mazamorra Morada to serving bowls or glasses and refrigerate until chilled.
10. Serve the Mazamorra Morada cold, garnished with ground cinnamon if desired.
11. Enjoy this sweet and comforting Peruvian dessert as a refreshing treat!

Mazamorra Morada can be enjoyed on its own or served with a side of rice pudding (arroz con leche) for a traditional Peruvian dessert experience.

Suspiro a la Limeña

Ingredients:

For the manjar blanco (dulce de leche):

- 2 cups whole milk
- 1 cup granulated sugar
- 1 cinnamon stick
- 1 teaspoon vanilla extract

For the meringue topping:

- 4 egg whites
- 1 cup granulated sugar
- 1/4 teaspoon cream of tartar

For garnish:

- Ground cinnamon or cinnamon sticks

Instructions:

1. Prepare the manjar blanco (dulce de leche):
    - In a saucepan, combine the whole milk, granulated sugar, and cinnamon stick over medium heat.
    - Stir continuously until the sugar has dissolved and the mixture comes to a gentle boil.
    - Reduce the heat to low and simmer, stirring occasionally, until the mixture thickens and reaches a caramel-like consistency, about 1 to 1.5 hours.
    - Remove from heat and stir in the vanilla extract. Let it cool completely.
2. Once the manjar blanco has cooled, pour it into individual serving glasses or a large serving dish, filling them halfway.
3. Prepare the meringue topping:
    - In a clean, dry mixing bowl, beat the egg whites with an electric mixer on medium speed until soft peaks form.

- Gradually add the granulated sugar and cream of tartar while continuing to beat the egg whites until stiff, glossy peaks form.
4. Spoon or pipe the meringue over the cooled manjar blanco in the serving glasses or dish, covering it completely.
5. Use a kitchen torch to lightly brown the tops of the meringue, creating a caramelized finish.
6. Alternatively, preheat your oven's broiler and place the glasses or dish under the broiler for a few seconds until the meringue is lightly browned.
7. Garnish each serving with a sprinkle of ground cinnamon or a cinnamon stick.
8. Refrigerate the Suspiro a la Limeña for at least 1 hour, or until chilled and set.
9. Serve cold and enjoy the creamy sweetness of this delightful Peruvian dessert!

Suspiro a la Limeña is best enjoyed chilled and makes for an elegant and indulgent treat that's sure to impress your guests.

Mazamorra de Calabaza

Ingredients:

- 1 lb (about 450g) pumpkin, peeled and diced
- 4 cups water
- 1 cinnamon stick
- 4 cloves
- 1 cup cornstarch
- 1 cup granulated sugar (adjust to taste)
- 1 teaspoon ground cinnamon
- 1 teaspoon vanilla extract
- Pinch of salt
- Raisins or chopped nuts for garnish (optional)

Instructions:

1. In a large pot, combine the diced pumpkin, water, cinnamon stick, and cloves. Bring to a boil over medium-high heat.
2. Reduce the heat to low and simmer the pumpkin until it's soft and tender, about 15-20 minutes.
3. Once the pumpkin is cooked, remove the cinnamon stick and cloves from the pot and discard them.
4. Using a potato masher or fork, mash the cooked pumpkin until smooth. You can also use a blender or food processor for a smoother consistency.
5. In a small bowl, dissolve the cornstarch in a little water to make a slurry.
6. Gradually pour the cornstarch slurry into the pot of mashed pumpkin, stirring constantly, until the mixture thickens.
7. Add the granulated sugar, ground cinnamon, vanilla extract, and a pinch of salt to the pot. Stir until the sugar is dissolved and the ingredients are well combined.
8. Continue to cook the Mazamorra de Calabaza over low heat, stirring constantly, for another 5-10 minutes, or until the mixture is thick and creamy.
9. Remove the pot from the heat and let the Mazamorra de Calabaza cool slightly.
10. Transfer the Mazamorra de Calabaza to serving bowls and garnish with raisins or chopped nuts if desired.
11. Serve the Mazamorra de Calabaza warm or chilled, depending on your preference.

12. Enjoy the comforting sweetness of this traditional Peruvian dessert!

Mazamorra de Calabaza is a delicious and comforting dessert that's perfect for enjoying on its own or as a topping for ice cream or yogurt. Feel free to adjust the sweetness and spices to suit your taste preferences.

Leche Asada

Ingredients:

- 4 cups (1 liter) whole milk
- 4 eggs
- 1 cup granulated sugar
- 1 teaspoon vanilla extract
- Ground cinnamon or lemon zest for flavoring (optional)
- Additional sugar for caramelizing the top

Instructions:

1. Preheat your oven to 350°F (175°C). Prepare a large baking dish or individual ramekins by greasing them lightly with butter or cooking spray.
2. In a saucepan, heat the milk over medium heat until it's hot but not boiling. Remove from heat and let it cool slightly.
3. In a large mixing bowl, beat the eggs with the sugar until well combined and slightly thickened.
4. Gradually pour the hot milk into the egg mixture, stirring constantly to prevent the eggs from scrambling. Stir in the vanilla extract and any optional flavorings, such as ground cinnamon or lemon zest.
5. Strain the mixture through a fine-mesh sieve to remove any lumps or air bubbles.
6. Pour the strained mixture into the prepared baking dish or ramekins.
7. Place the baking dish or ramekins in a larger baking pan and carefully add hot water to the outer pan, creating a water bath (bain-marie) that comes halfway up the sides of the baking dish or ramekins.
8. Bake the Leche Asada in the preheated oven for about 45-60 minutes, or until set and lightly golden on top. The exact baking time will depend on the size and depth of your baking dish or ramekins.
9. Once the Leche Asada is set, remove it from the oven and let it cool to room temperature. Then refrigerate it for at least a few hours or overnight to chill and set completely.
10. Before serving, sprinkle a thin layer of granulated sugar evenly over the top of the Leche Asada. Use a kitchen torch to caramelize the sugar until it forms a golden-brown crust.

11. Alternatively, you can place the Leche Asada under the broiler for a few minutes until the sugar caramelizes.
12. Serve the Leche Asada chilled, either directly from the baking dish or unmolded onto serving plates.
13. Enjoy the creamy, caramelized goodness of this classic Latin American dessert!

Leche Asada is best enjoyed chilled, and its creamy texture and caramelized top make it a delightful treat for any occasion.

Turrón de Doña Pepa

Ingredients:

For the anise cookies:

- 4 cups all-purpose flour
- 1 tablespoon anise seeds
- 1 tablespoon anise extract
- 1 teaspoon baking powder
- Pinch of salt
- 1 cup unsalted butter, at room temperature
- 1 cup granulated sugar
- 2 eggs
- Zest of 1 orange

For the syrup:

- 2 cups chancaca (piloncillo or panela can be used as substitutes)
- 1 cup water
- 1 cinnamon stick
- 1 tablespoon anise seeds

For decoration:

- Colorful candy sprinkles
- Candied fruit (such as orange and lemon peel)
- Small candies or chocolate chips

Instructions:

1. Preheat your oven to 350°F (175°C). Line a baking sheet with parchment paper or grease it lightly.
2. In a bowl, whisk together the flour, anise seeds, baking powder, and salt. Set aside.

3. In another bowl, cream together the butter and sugar until light and fluffy. Add the eggs one at a time, beating well after each addition. Stir in the anise extract and orange zest.
4. Gradually add the dry ingredients to the wet ingredients, mixing until a dough forms. If the dough is too dry, you can add a little milk, one tablespoon at a time, until it comes together.
5. Roll out the dough on a floured surface to about 1/4 inch (6 mm) thickness. Use cookie cutters to cut out shapes, such as rectangles or circles.
6. Place the cookies on the prepared baking sheet and bake in the preheated oven for 10-12 minutes, or until lightly golden around the edges. Remove from the oven and let them cool completely.
7. While the cookies are cooling, prepare the syrup. In a saucepan, combine the chancaca, water, cinnamon stick, and anise seeds. Bring to a boil over medium heat, then reduce the heat and simmer for about 10-15 minutes, or until the syrup thickens slightly. Remove from heat and let it cool.
8. Once the cookies and syrup are cool, assemble the Turrón de Doña Pepa. Dip each cookie into the syrup, coating it well, then stack them on top of each other to form layers. Repeat this process until you have a tall stack of cookies.
9. Pour any remaining syrup over the top of the stack, allowing it to drizzle down the sides.
10. Decorate the Turrón de Doña Pepa with colorful candy sprinkles, candied fruit, and small candies or chocolate chips.
11. Let the Turrón de Doña Pepa sit for a few hours or overnight to allow the flavors to meld together and the syrup to set.
12. Slice the Turrón de Doña Pepa into individual servings and enjoy this festive Peruvian treat!

Turrón de Doña Pepa is a delightful combination of sweet, crunchy cookies and sticky syrup, with a burst of color and flavor from the decorations. It's a perfect dessert for celebrating special occasions or sharing with loved ones.

Alfajores

Ingredients:

For the cookies:

- 1 cup (225g) unsalted butter, softened
- 1/2 cup (100g) granulated sugar
- 2 egg yolks
- 1 teaspoon vanilla extract
- 2 cups (250g) all-purpose flour
- 1/2 cup (60g) cornstarch
- 1 teaspoon baking powder
- 1/4 teaspoon salt

For assembly and decoration:

- Dulce de leche (store-bought or homemade)
- Powdered sugar, for dusting
- Shredded coconut (optional)

Instructions:

1. Preheat your oven to 350°F (175°C). Line a baking sheet with parchment paper.
2. In a large mixing bowl, cream together the softened butter and granulated sugar until light and fluffy.
3. Add the egg yolks and vanilla extract to the butter-sugar mixture, and beat until well combined.
4. In a separate bowl, sift together the all-purpose flour, cornstarch, baking powder, and salt.
5. Gradually add the dry ingredients to the wet ingredients, mixing until a soft dough forms.
6. Roll out the dough on a floured surface to about 1/4 inch (6 mm) thickness. Use a round cookie cutter to cut out cookies.

7. Place the cookies onto the prepared baking sheet, leaving some space between each one.
8. Bake the cookies in the preheated oven for 10-12 minutes, or until lightly golden around the edges. Remove from the oven and let them cool completely on a wire rack.
9. Once the cookies are cool, spread a generous amount of dulce de leche onto the bottom side of one cookie, then sandwich it with another cookie to form an Alfajor.
10. Repeat this process with the remaining cookies and dulce de leche.
11. Optional: Roll the edges of the assembled Alfajores in shredded coconut for extra flavor and decoration.
12. Dust the tops of the Alfajores with powdered sugar using a fine-mesh sieve.
13. Serve the Alfajores immediately, or store them in an airtight container for up to several days.

These Alfajores are a delightful treat with their buttery cookies and sweet dulce de leche filling. They're perfect for enjoying with a cup of coffee or tea, or for sharing with friends and family during special occasions.

Picarones

Ingredients:

For the picarones:

- 1 cup mashed sweet potatoes
- 1 cup mashed pumpkin
- 2 cups all-purpose flour
- 1 packet (7g) active dry yeast
- 1/4 cup warm water
- 1 tablespoon granulated sugar
- 1 teaspoon ground anise
- 1 teaspoon ground cinnamon
- 1/4 teaspoon salt
- Vegetable oil for frying

For the chancaca syrup:

- 2 cups chancaca (piloncillo or panela can be used as substitutes)
- 2 cups water
- 1 cinnamon stick
- 4 cloves
- 1 teaspoon grated orange zest (optional)

Instructions:

1. In a small bowl, dissolve the yeast and granulated sugar in warm water. Let it sit for about 5-10 minutes, or until it becomes frothy.
2. In a large mixing bowl, combine the mashed sweet potatoes, mashed pumpkin, all-purpose flour, ground anise, ground cinnamon, and salt. Mix well.
3. Add the yeast mixture to the dough and knead until it forms a smooth, elastic dough. Cover the bowl with a clean kitchen towel and let the dough rise in a warm place for about 1-2 hours, or until it doubles in size.
4. While the dough is rising, prepare the chancaca syrup. In a saucepan, combine the chancaca, water, cinnamon stick, cloves, and grated orange zest (if using). Bring to a boil over medium heat, then reduce the heat and simmer for about

10-15 minutes, or until the syrup thickens slightly. Remove from heat and let it cool.
5. Once the dough has risen, heat vegetable oil in a deep fryer or large pot to 350°F (175°C).
6. Using wet hands to prevent sticking, shape the dough into small rings or figures, about 2-3 inches (5-7 cm) in diameter.
7. Carefully place the shaped picarones into the hot oil, frying them in batches until they are golden brown and cooked through, about 3-4 minutes per side.
8. Remove the fried picarones from the oil using a slotted spoon and drain them on paper towels to remove excess oil.
9. Serve the picarones warm, drizzled with the prepared chancaca syrup.
10. Enjoy these delicious Peruvian picarones as a sweet and comforting treat!

Picarones are best enjoyed fresh and warm, straight from the fryer, with the aromatic chancaca syrup adding a delightful sweetness to the soft and pillowy dough.

Frejol Colado

Ingredients:

- 1 cup dried black beans (frejoles negros)
- 1 cup white rice
- 8 cups water
- 4 cups whole milk
- 1 cup granulated sugar or panela, grated
- 1 cinnamon stick
- 1 teaspoon vanilla extract
- Pinch of salt
- Ground cinnamon for garnish (optional)

Instructions:

1. Rinse the black beans under cold water to remove any dirt or debris. Place them in a large pot with 4 cups of water and bring to a boil over medium-high heat.
2. Once boiling, reduce the heat to low and simmer the black beans, partially covered, for about 1 to 1.5 hours, or until they are very soft and starting to fall apart. Add more water if necessary to keep the beans covered.
3. While the black beans are cooking, rinse the rice under cold water until the water runs clear. Drain well.
4. In another pot, combine the rice with 4 cups of water and bring to a boil over medium-high heat. Reduce the heat to low, cover, and simmer for about 15-20 minutes, or until the rice is cooked and the water is absorbed.
5. In a blender or food processor, puree the cooked black beans with their cooking liquid until smooth. You may need to do this in batches.
6. In a large saucepan, combine the pureed black beans, cooked rice, whole milk, sugar or grated panela, cinnamon stick, vanilla extract, and a pinch of salt. Stir well to combine.
7. Cook the mixture over medium heat, stirring frequently, until it thickens to a creamy consistency, about 20-30 minutes.
8. Remove the cinnamon stick from the mixture and discard.
9. Serve the frejol colado warm or chilled, garnished with ground cinnamon if desired.
10. Enjoy this comforting and nutritious Peruvian dessert as a sweet treat or snack!

Frejol colado is a hearty and satisfying dessert, perfect for enjoying on its own or with a sprinkle of ground cinnamon on top. It's a great way to incorporate beans into your diet in a delicious and unexpected way.

Cau Cau

Ingredients:

- 1 lb (about 450g) beef tripe (panza de res), cleaned and diced (or substitute with chicken breast, diced)
- 2 tablespoons vegetable oil
- 1 onion, finely chopped
- 2 cloves garlic, minced
- 1-2 aji amarillo peppers, seeded and finely chopped (or substitute with aji amarillo paste)
- 1 teaspoon ground turmeric
- 2 medium potatoes, peeled and diced
- 2 cups beef or chicken broth
- Salt and pepper to taste
- 2 hard-boiled eggs, sliced (for garnish)
- Black olives (for garnish)
- Chopped fresh cilantro or parsley (for garnish)

Instructions:

1. If using beef tripe, clean it thoroughly under cold running water and cut it into small, bite-sized pieces. If using chicken breast, dice it into bite-sized pieces.
2. In a large pot or Dutch oven, heat the vegetable oil over medium heat. Add the chopped onion and cook until soft and translucent, about 3-5 minutes.
3. Add the minced garlic and chopped aji amarillo peppers to the pot, and cook for another 2-3 minutes, stirring frequently.
4. Stir in the ground turmeric and cook for an additional minute to toast the spices.
5. Add the diced beef tripe or chicken to the pot and cook until browned on all sides, about 5-7 minutes.
6. Once the meat is browned, add the diced potatoes to the pot, followed by the beef or chicken broth. Bring the mixture to a simmer.
7. Cover the pot and cook over low heat for about 20-25 minutes, or until the potatoes are tender and the meat is cooked through. If the sauce becomes too thick, you can add more broth or water as needed.
8. Season the cau cau with salt and pepper to taste.
9. To serve, ladle the cau cau into individual bowls or plates. Garnish each serving with slices of hard-boiled egg, black olives, and chopped fresh cilantro or parsley.

10. Enjoy your homemade cau cau with a side of rice or crusty bread!

Cau Cau is a flavorful and comforting dish that's perfect for warming up on a chilly day. The combination of tender meat, creamy potatoes, and aromatic spices makes it a favorite in Peruvian cuisine.

Tacacho con Cuy

Ingredients:

For the Tacacho:

- 4 green plantains, peeled and chopped
- 1/2 cup lard or vegetable oil for frying
- Salt to taste

For the Cuy:

- 1 or 2 whole guinea pigs, cleaned and gutted
- Salt and pepper to taste
- 1 tablespoon vegetable oil

For the Salsa:

- 2 red onions, finely chopped
- 2 tomatoes, diced
- 1/4 cup chopped cilantro
- 2 tablespoons lime juice
- Salt and pepper to taste

Instructions:

1. Prepare the Tacacho:
    - Boil the chopped green plantains in salted water until tender, about 15-20 minutes.
    - Drain the cooked plantains and mash them in a bowl until smooth.
    - Form the mashed plantains into small patties or balls.
2. Heat the lard or vegetable oil in a skillet over medium heat. Fry the Tacacho patties or balls until golden brown and crispy on the outside, about 3-4 minutes per side. Remove from the skillet and drain on paper towels.

3. Prepare the Cuy:
    - Preheat your grill or oven to medium-high heat.
    - Season the guinea pigs with salt and pepper, inside and out.
    - Rub the vegetable oil all over the guinea pigs.
    - Grill or roast the guinea pigs for about 30-40 minutes, turning occasionally, until cooked through and golden brown. The internal temperature should reach 165°F (74°C).
    - Remove the guinea pigs from the grill or oven and let them rest for a few minutes before serving.
4. Prepare the Salsa:
    - In a bowl, combine the chopped red onions, diced tomatoes, chopped cilantro, lime juice, salt, and pepper. Mix well to combine.
5. To serve, place a Tacacho patty or ball on a plate, along with a portion of grilled or roasted guinea pig. Serve with the salsa on the side.
6. Enjoy your Tacacho con cuy, a traditional and flavorful dish from the Peruvian Amazon region!

Tacacho con cuy is a hearty and satisfying dish that showcases the unique flavors and ingredients of the Peruvian Amazon. It's a must-try for adventurous foodies looking to experience authentic Peruvian cuisine.

Arroz Zambito

Ingredients:

- 1 cup white rice
- 2 cups water
- 1 cinnamon stick
- 2 cloves
- 1 cup chancaca (piloncillo or panela can be used as substitutes)
- 2 cups evaporated milk
- 1 teaspoon vanilla extract
- Ground cinnamon for garnish

Instructions:

1. Rinse the rice under cold water until the water runs clear. Drain well.
2. In a medium saucepan, combine the rinsed rice with 2 cups of water, cinnamon stick, and cloves. Bring to a boil over medium-high heat.
3. Reduce the heat to low, cover the saucepan, and simmer the rice until it's tender and the water is absorbed, about 15-20 minutes.
4. While the rice is cooking, prepare the chancaca syrup. In a separate saucepan, combine the chancaca with enough water to cover it. Bring to a boil over medium heat, stirring occasionally, until the chancaca is completely dissolved and the syrup thickens slightly, about 10-15 minutes.
5. Once the rice is cooked, remove the cinnamon stick and cloves from the saucepan and discard them.
6. Add the evaporated milk and vanilla extract to the cooked rice, stirring to combine.
7. Gradually pour the prepared chancaca syrup into the rice mixture, stirring constantly, until it reaches your desired level of sweetness. You may not need to use all of the syrup, depending on your taste preferences.
8. Continue to cook the rice mixture over low heat, stirring frequently, until it thickens to a creamy consistency, about 10-15 minutes.
9. Remove the saucepan from the heat and let the Arroz Zambito cool slightly.
10. Serve the Arroz Zambito warm or chilled, garnished with a sprinkle of ground cinnamon on top.
11. Enjoy this delicious and comforting Peruvian dessert!

Arroz Zambito is a wonderful treat that's perfect for enjoying on its own or as a sweet ending to a Peruvian meal. Its rich caramel flavor and creamy texture make it a favorite among dessert lovers.

Mazamorra de Quinua

Ingredients:

- 1 cup quinoa, rinsed
- 4 cups water
- 1 cinnamon stick
- 4 cloves
- 1 cup evaporated milk
- 1/2 cup granulated sugar (adjust to taste)
- 1 teaspoon vanilla extract
- Ground cinnamon for garnish (optional)

Instructions:

1. In a large saucepan, combine the rinsed quinoa, water, cinnamon stick, and cloves. Bring to a boil over medium-high heat.
2. Once boiling, reduce the heat to low and simmer the quinoa, partially covered, for about 15-20 minutes, or until it's cooked and the water is absorbed. Stir occasionally to prevent sticking.
3. While the quinoa is cooking, prepare the sweetened milk mixture. In a separate saucepan, combine the evaporated milk, granulated sugar, and vanilla extract. Heat over medium heat, stirring occasionally, until the sugar is completely dissolved and the mixture is warmed through.
4. Once the quinoa is cooked, remove the cinnamon stick and cloves from the saucepan and discard them.
5. Pour the sweetened milk mixture into the cooked quinoa, stirring to combine. Cook over low heat for an additional 5-10 minutes, allowing the flavors to meld together and the mixture to thicken slightly.
6. Remove the saucepan from the heat and let the Mazamorra de Quinua cool slightly.
7. Serve the Mazamorra de Quinua warm or chilled, garnished with a sprinkle of ground cinnamon on top if desired.
8. Enjoy this nutritious and comforting Peruvian dessert as a sweet treat or snack!

Mazamorra de Quinua is a wonderful way to enjoy the nutritional benefits of quinoa in a sweet and satisfying dessert. It's perfect for serving during special occasions or as a comforting treat on a chilly day.

Ensalada de Pallares

Ingredients:

- 2 cups cooked pallares beans (lima beans), drained and rinsed
- 1 red onion, finely chopped
- 2 tomatoes, diced
- 1/4 cup chopped fresh cilantro
- 2 tablespoons lime juice
- 2 tablespoons olive oil
- Salt and pepper to taste
- Optional: sliced avocado for garnish

Instructions:

1. In a large mixing bowl, combine the cooked pallares beans, chopped red onion, diced tomatoes, and chopped fresh cilantro.
2. In a small bowl, whisk together the lime juice and olive oil to make the dressing. Season with salt and pepper to taste.
3. Pour the dressing over the salad ingredients in the large mixing bowl.
4. Gently toss the salad until all the ingredients are well combined and evenly coated with the dressing.
5. Taste and adjust the seasoning with additional salt, pepper, or lime juice if needed.
6. Optional: Garnish the Ensalada de Pallares with slices of avocado before serving.
7. Serve the Ensalada de Pallares chilled or at room temperature as a refreshing side dish or appetizer.

Ensalada de Pallares is a light and flavorful salad that pairs well with grilled meats, seafood, or other Peruvian dishes. It's perfect for serving at picnics, barbecues, or as a side dish for a casual meal with family and friends. Enjoy!

Tamales Peruanos

Ingredients:

For the masa (dough):

- 2 cups masa harina (corn flour for tamales)
- 1 cup chicken or vegetable broth
- 1/2 cup lard or vegetable shortening
- 1 teaspoon baking powder
- Salt to taste

For the filling:

- 2 cups cooked and shredded chicken or pork
- 1 onion, finely chopped
- 2 cloves garlic, minced
- 1 tablespoon vegetable oil
- 1 teaspoon ground cumin
- 1 teaspoon paprika
- Salt and pepper to taste
- Sliced olives, hard-boiled eggs, raisins, and/or roasted peppers (optional)

For assembling:

- Banana leaves, softened and cut into squares
- Kitchen twine or strips of banana leaf for tying

Instructions:

1. Prepare the masa: In a mixing bowl, combine the masa harina, chicken or vegetable broth, lard or vegetable shortening, baking powder, and salt. Mix until a smooth dough forms. If the dough is too dry, add more broth, one tablespoon at a time, until it reaches a spreadable consistency.

2. Prepare the filling: In a skillet, heat the vegetable oil over medium heat. Add the chopped onion and garlic, and cook until softened, about 3-5 minutes. Add the shredded chicken or pork, ground cumin, paprika, salt, and pepper. Cook, stirring occasionally, until the meat is heated through and well-coated with the spices. Remove from heat and let it cool slightly.
3. Assemble the tamales: Place a banana leaf square on a clean work surface. Spread a thin layer of masa dough in the center of the banana leaf, leaving about a 2-inch border on all sides. Spoon a portion of the filling onto the center of the masa dough. Add any optional ingredients, such as sliced olives, hard-boiled eggs, raisins, or roasted peppers, if desired.
4. Fold the sides of the banana leaf over the filling to enclose it completely. Fold the top and bottom edges of the banana leaf over the center to form a rectangular package. Tie the tamales securely with kitchen twine or strips of banana leaf to keep them closed.
5. Repeat the process with the remaining masa dough and filling until all the ingredients are used.
6. Steam the tamales: Arrange the assembled tamales in a steamer basket, standing them upright with the folded edge facing down. Fill the bottom of the steamer pot with water, making sure it doesn't touch the tamales. Cover the steamer pot with a lid and steam the tamales over medium heat for about 1 to 1.5 hours, or until the masa dough is firm and cooked through.
7. Remove the tamales from the steamer and let them cool slightly before serving. Serve the Tamales Peruanos warm, unwrapping them from the banana leaves before eating.

Enjoy the delicious flavors of Tamales Peruanos, a classic Peruvian dish that's perfect for sharing with family and friends!

Ensalada de Chonta

Ingredients:

- 1 can (14 ounces) hearts of palm, drained and sliced
- 1 red bell pepper, thinly sliced
- 1 yellow bell pepper, thinly sliced
- 1 green bell pepper, thinly sliced
- 1 small red onion, thinly sliced
- 1 tomato, diced
- 1/4 cup chopped fresh cilantro
- 2 tablespoons olive oil
- 2 tablespoons lime juice
- Salt and pepper to taste

Instructions:

1. In a large mixing bowl, combine the sliced hearts of palm, sliced bell peppers, sliced red onion, diced tomato, and chopped fresh cilantro.
2. In a small bowl, whisk together the olive oil and lime juice to make the dressing. Season with salt and pepper to taste.
3. Pour the dressing over the salad ingredients in the large mixing bowl.
4. Gently toss the salad until all the ingredients are well combined and evenly coated with the dressing.
5. Taste and adjust the seasoning with additional salt, pepper, or lime juice if needed.
6. Optional: Garnish the Ensalada de Chonta with additional chopped cilantro before serving.
7. Serve the Ensalada de Chonta chilled or at room temperature as a refreshing side dish or appetizer.

Ensalada de Chonta is a light and flavorful salad that pairs well with grilled meats, seafood, or other Latin American dishes. It's perfect for serving at picnics, barbecues, or as a side dish for a casual meal with family and friends. Enjoy!

Crema Volteada

Ingredients:

For the caramel sauce:

- 1 cup granulated sugar
- 1/4 cup water

For the custard:

- 4 eggs
- 1 can (14 oz) sweetened condensed milk
- 1 can (12 oz) evaporated milk
- 1 teaspoon vanilla extract

Instructions:

1. Preheat your oven to 350°F (175°C). Place a roasting pan filled with about 1 inch of hot water on the bottom rack of the oven. This will create a water bath for baking the custard.
2. To make the caramel sauce, add the granulated sugar and water to a small saucepan. Heat over medium-high heat, stirring constantly, until the sugar dissolves and the mixture comes to a boil.
3. Reduce the heat to medium-low and let the mixture simmer without stirring. Swirl the pan occasionally to ensure even caramelization. Cook until the mixture turns a deep amber color, about 5-7 minutes.
4. Once the caramel reaches the desired color, immediately pour it into a round cake pan or baking dish, tilting the pan to coat the bottom evenly. Be careful as the caramel will be extremely hot. Set aside to cool and harden.
5. In a blender, combine the eggs, sweetened condensed milk, evaporated milk, and vanilla extract. Blend until smooth and well combined.
6. Pour the custard mixture over the cooled caramel in the cake pan.

7. Carefully place the cake pan in the preheated oven, on the rack above the roasting pan filled with hot water. Bake for 45-50 minutes, or until the custard is set around the edges but still slightly jiggly in the center.
8. Remove the cake pan from the oven and let it cool to room temperature. Once cooled, cover the pan with plastic wrap and refrigerate for at least 4 hours, or preferably overnight, to chill and set completely.
9. To serve, run a knife around the edges of the cake pan to loosen the custard. Place a serving platter or plate on top of the pan, then quickly and carefully invert the pan to release the Crema Volteada onto the platter. The caramel sauce will flow over the custard.
10. Slice and serve the Crema Volteada chilled, garnished with additional caramel sauce if desired.

Crema Volteada is a delightful dessert with its silky-smooth custard and rich caramel flavor. It's sure to be a hit at any gathering or special occasion!

Sopa a la Criolla

Ingredients:

- 1 lb (450g) beef sirloin, thinly sliced
- 8 cups beef broth
- 1 cup vermicelli noodles
- 1 large red onion, thinly sliced
- 2 tomatoes, diced
- 2 cloves garlic, minced
- 1 tablespoon vegetable oil
- 1 tablespoon aji panca paste (Peruvian red chili paste), or substitute with aji amarillo paste
- 1 teaspoon ground cumin
- 1 teaspoon dried oregano
- 1/4 cup chopped fresh cilantro
- 1/4 cup chopped fresh parsley
- 2 eggs
- Juice of 1 lime
- Salt and pepper to taste

Instructions:

1. In a large pot, heat the vegetable oil over medium heat. Add the sliced onions and minced garlic, and cook until softened, about 3-5 minutes.
2. Add the sliced beef to the pot and cook until browned on all sides, about 5-7 minutes.
3. Stir in the diced tomatoes, aji panca paste (or aji amarillo paste), ground cumin, and dried oregano. Cook for another 2-3 minutes, until the tomatoes start to soften.
4. Pour the beef broth into the pot and bring the mixture to a boil.
5. Once boiling, reduce the heat to low and simmer the soup, partially covered, for about 15-20 minutes to allow the flavors to meld together.
6. Meanwhile, in a separate pot, cook the vermicelli noodles according to the package instructions. Drain and set aside.
7. In a small bowl, beat the eggs with the juice of 1 lime. Slowly pour the beaten eggs into the simmering soup, stirring gently to create egg ribbons.

8. Add the cooked vermicelli noodles to the soup and stir to combine. Cook for another 2-3 minutes to heat through.
9. Season the soup with salt and pepper to taste. Stir in the chopped fresh cilantro and parsley.
10. Ladle the Sopa a la Criolla into individual serving bowls and serve hot.

Sopa a la Criolla is often served with aji rocoto sauce or fresh chili peppers on the side for those who enjoy extra heat. It's a delicious and comforting dish that's sure to become a favorite in your home!

Yuca a la Huancaína

Ingredients:

For the Huancaína sauce:

- 1 cup feta cheese, crumbled (or substitute with queso fresco)
- 1/2 cup evaporated milk
- 2-3 yellow Peruvian aji amarillo peppers, seeded and deveined
- 2 cloves garlic
- 1/4 cup vegetable oil
- 4-6 saltine crackers (or substitute with bread crumbs)
- Salt to taste

For the yuca:

- 2 lbs (about 1 kg) yuca (cassava), peeled and cut into large chunks
- Water for boiling
- Salt for boiling

For garnish (optional):

- Hard-boiled eggs, sliced
- Black olives
- Fresh parsley or cilantro, chopped

Instructions:

1. Prepare the Huancaína sauce:
    - In a blender or food processor, combine the crumbled feta cheese, evaporated milk, yellow Peruvian aji amarillo peppers, garlic cloves, vegetable oil, and saltine crackers (or bread crumbs). Blend until smooth and creamy. If the sauce is too thick, you can add a little more evaporated milk to reach your desired consistency. Taste and adjust the seasoning with salt if needed.
2. Prepare the yuca:

- Place the peeled and cut yuca chunks in a large pot and cover them with water. Add a generous pinch of salt to the water.
    - Bring the water to a boil over medium-high heat, then reduce the heat to medium-low and simmer the yuca for about 20-25 minutes, or until fork-tender.
    - Once the yuca is cooked, drain it well and let it cool slightly.
3. To serve:
    - Arrange the boiled yuca on a serving platter or individual plates.
    - Generously spoon the Huancaína sauce over the yuca.
    - If desired, garnish with slices of hard-boiled eggs, black olives, and chopped fresh parsley or cilantro.
4. Serve the Yuca a la Huancaína immediately, while still warm.

Yuca a la Huancaína is a flavorful and comforting dish that's perfect for sharing with family and friends. The creamy and spicy Huancaína sauce pairs beautifully with the tender yuca, creating a satisfying and memorable meal. Enjoy!

Pisco Sour

Ingredients:

- 2 oz (60 ml) Pisco
- 1 oz (30 ml) fresh lime juice
- 3/4 oz (22 ml) simple syrup (equal parts sugar and water, dissolved)
- 1 egg white
- Angostura bitters
- Ice cubes

Instructions:

1. In a cocktail shaker, combine the Pisco, fresh lime juice, simple syrup, and egg white.
2. Add a handful of ice cubes to the shaker.
3. Shake vigorously for about 10-15 seconds to froth up the egg white and chill the mixture.
4. Strain the cocktail into a chilled rocks glass or cocktail glass filled with ice.
5. Garnish the Pisco Sour with a few drops of Angostura bitters on top.
6. Optionally, you can garnish with a slice of lime or a cherry.
7. Serve immediately and enjoy your delicious Pisco Sour!

Pisco Sour is a delightful cocktail with a perfect balance of sweet, sour, and boozy flavors. It's a great drink to enjoy on its own or paired with Peruvian cuisine. Cheers!

www.ingramcontent.com/pod-product-compliance
Lightning Source LLC
LaVergne TN
LVHW062047070526
838201LV00080B/2108